www.finishinglinepress.com

IRONWEED

poems by

Jackie Ison Kalbli

Finishing Line Press
Georgetown, Kentucky

IRONWEED

Dedicated to my parents,
Jack Ferguson Ison and Cleo Adkins Ison

"They say on yonder's side of where those muddy waters flow,
A man can make a dollar a day across the Ohio."

Dale Farmer, Across the Ohio
The Mountain Minor

ACKNOWLEDGMENTS

"Pioneers" is a revision of a poem previously published in *Pine Mountain Sand & Gravel*

Pioneers epigraph, "When hurt is all that's handed down, you learn to claim it." Is from Pauletta Hansel's book *Heartbreak Tree*

"The Burial" poem lyrics are from the Christian hymn "Softly and Tenderly," a classic invitational written by Will Lamartine Thompson in 1880. Public Domain.

My father's poem, "The Nation's Construction Crew," was first published in a journal of the Pipefitters Union sometime in the 1950s. The complete citation is unknown.

The poem "Corn" appeared in the anthology *I Thought I Heard A Cardinal Sing Ohio's Appalachian Voices*.

"Lying on my back on Robert Frost's grave" appeared in *Common Threads*

The epigraph from the poem "Ironweed" Is from the *The Wild Iris*, by Louise Glück.

The lyrics from the song "Across the Ohio" were borrowed from the movie *The Mountain Minor*.

Publisher: Leah Huete de Maines
Editor: Christen Kincaid
Cover Art: Becki Ison
Author Photo: Ron Stevens
Cover Design: Elizabeth Maines McCleavy

Order online: www.finishinglinepress.com
also available on amazon.com

Author inquiries and mail orders:
Finishing Line Press
PO Box 1626
Georgetown, Kentucky 40324
USA

Contents

Girl as Migrant

Greasy wolf teeth man
pumped the gas
stuck his sweaty head

through the back window of
my parents' 1955 Ford—
stinky hot breath in my face.

You're so cute I would like to adopt you.
Why don't you come home with me?

I felt disposable and feared
being given to an orphanage.
I expected my mother to say

I would never let anyone take you.
But she didn't speak.

When I visited Kentucky kin,
I hinted at them to keep me.

I would be a helpful girl
to Uncle Danny and
milk cows of a morning.

Be loved to pluck tomatoes
and holler in the family
for beans and cornbread at noon.

Pioneers

> "When hurt is all that's handed down you learn to claim it."
> —Pauletta Hansel, *Heartbreak Tree*

The WPA camped out men and boys
from the hollers of Elliott County,
ending the Great Depression.
Families ate again.
World War II and Oak Ridge
drew workers from mountains.
There were places to go!

Mom and Dad, in 1950's garb
cracked open a fresh can of fate,
crossed the Ohio where
jobs were tomatoes on the vine,
but they dragged along their
suitcase of struggles.

I am born and raised North,
marinaded in all that's Kentucky, a
constant hunger for home biting
behind polished teeth,

making stubbed-toed poor
in a tobacco barn,
seem like Beverly Hills.

Elliott County Girl

After a photo of my mother and father at a bus station heading
to a job at the Manhattan Project: Oak Ridge, TN, 1942

Poverty to Progress who
could not want more—
jobs jobs jobs!

Waves of hair roll high across her forehead
eyes kissing me ten years
before I was born and now
forty-six years after her death.

To the girl I see,
I am daughter
I am mother
I am grandmother.

Knowing the end of the story, I would warn her:

You will raise five children
alone, away from home,
and die young!

Which voice would answer—
girl mother ghost?

I can hear her shirk denial—

Honey, I flicked Kentucky off like a fly on the screen door.

Clearing Space for D.H. Lawrence

The mountain road offers no orienting features or historical markers.
The car slips on rolling gravel in creepy pine darkness,
  then an opening appears for his small homestead.

I find the crypt on a trail,
wide open, doors warped,
his tomb in disarray—

leaves, cones, cobwebs,
feathers, a dented Coke can
and a Clark Bar wrapper.
A stubby broom rests in a tight corner,
handle flecked with mint green paint
straw apron worn short.

I bow, I sweep, we talk.
He says he misses his typewriter, pencils, friends—
wants to know who is reading
Lady Chatterley these days.
I respond *it was written in a different time.*

He whines I forget concepts from life.
What is time?

I try changing the subject.
How do you like death?
Has it evolved?
Improved perhaps?

Spiders, bits of fur, dust are
airborne in a cleaning frenzy.
Out flies a corpse sparrow.

I so enjoy when the dead talk.

Lying on my back on Robert Frost's grave,

I wondered if my head was
on his head or on his feet.

He listened while I explained my learning
of apples hired men, snow.

I longed to flip over and hug him,
but his daughter, son, wife
are buried around—
I didn't want to cause family problems.

When I was very young, he read on TV.
My mother, fading in a flannel gown
spoke from a flowered sofa:
Remember this man
he will be gone when you are grown.
Remember his words and sounds.

Decades before I was grown
he died, along with my father, JFK and
MLK in a downward spiral of endings.

So, I memorized his words and sounds
because she rarely gave advice.

I remember her for this wisdom,
but her life disappeared into the florals,
blooming as a forget-me-not.

Dad at 44

Sprawled in the Big Chair
scrutinizing scribbles on an
Aviator brand, top bound paper pad,
with a childlike blue airplane zooming
across the orange cover.

He wordled on envelopes
book margins and smoke packs
featuring a hairy brown camel at an
oasis with a pyramid and palm tree.

His pencil sharpened with a
World War II pocket knife,
was a dull stump.

I didn't know why he sat all day.
I knew things should be done, like
mowing, or reading *Peter Rabbit*.

He shifted a bit for comfort,
glasses held with first aid tape.

When he was 46,
a truck crushed his head.

I hoarded his shattered glasses
in a chocolate box for 51 years.

The Deal

In morning rain, groaning Truck heaved onto Road. Daddy's 1960 Ford & Faith crossed fingers. It was a school day in September. Ford & Faith crossed fingers. We were moving in two weeks! A school day in September. Truck & Rain dealing. Overjoy a new house! Mommy asked me if blue or green carpet was best. Joy, a new home! I'm nine in 4th grade. Mom asked blue or green carpet? Truck & Rain made The Deal. Nine in 4th grade. I'm feeling my Cheerios! I waved goodbye to Daddy. I'm a Cheerio! I called out *I'll kiss you tonight*! I goodbye wave. Did he see me? I called out *I will hug you tonight*...I think he waved back. Did he see me? At school, rain. I think he waved back. Daddy driving in rain, going to work. I was taught to love a good thunderstorm.

Mommy is packing papers on the floor. Daddy driving in rain, going to work. Papers scattered, abandoned, walked on. Truck roaring down Slick Curve. Mommy packing. Did Rain or Truck warn Dad? Give him a chance? He is caught in the windshield. His screams are like thunder!

My parents taught me to love a good thunderstorm.

Isonville Elementary, 1960

The undertaker dabbed at the
embalming fluid trickling
from Daddy's mouth,
school closed for the funeral.

A coffin in the gym didn't seem strange.
The town was named after
Great-Great Grandaddy Archibald,
so it belonged to me.

Praying, singing wailing
reached harmonic majesty in heaven.
A red-haired cousin
preached himself into a slather.

Mommy held me up:
*It's time to say goodbye to your daddy
for the last time.*

Up-North,
the place where I lived,
nobody ever heard of Isonville
or cared about what happened
to me that day at the school.

The Burial

I'm a raging shiver in a royal blue dress.
I kept the hand of my little brother, our
shoes sinking in yellow Kentucky clay as
we climb the mountain.

Dad, carried by his brothers
and his oldest son.

In the dusty procession following the casket—
hymns, calls, and responses—

> *Softly and Tenderly*
> *Jesus is calling*
> *Calling for you and for me…*

The Commandments said,
Honor thy father and thy mother.

Too late now to be good.
I prayed for another chance
but knew what death was.

A sullen sky stewed a mood.
Autumn sighed a swirl of seeds.

> *Calling all sinners*
> *come home, come home*
> *Ye who are weary come home.*

Posthumous Poetry Reading

The Nations Construction Crew
by Jack F. Ison
Cincinnati 1957

Red steel beams ripe for binding,
hoisted at the signal of men on the framework.

Engines wrench and clash
a foreman's frenzied
shouting heard above chaos.

Nail, bolt, stud, weld.
Sweat shirtless.
We are construction men.

From the tower, we can see
Kentucky across the Ohio.
Barges on the glistening water
slip south.

We are always on top,
inside or under, scrambling.

We repair the past
and break ground into the century.
Building what growls within.

We are the muscle of cement
and iron. Screwdrivers, bulldozers,
and cranes are toys.

We are construction men.

The Story of the Writer and the Typist

Short fingers wobble above home keys
small hands hunch like a hostage.

After the strike, a typing eraser brush
leaves holes in the paper and
spreads rubbery
balls across the dark oak table.

She painted the table gray after he died—
upcycled the matching buffet as a
posh dressing table for us girls—
reliable fashion-forward
green and lavender paisley skirt
ruffles brass upholstery nails.

Night Clerk at the Hotel Baxter, 1974

Drunks and prostitutes rent all the rooms.
My regrets to families who drive late
coming or going from Yellowstone.

At 2 a.m., the bar closes.
I stay awake by reading Lewis and Clark Journals
Shakespearean Sonnets and *Debbi Does Dallas*.

At four a.m. I abandon my post
slip between antique brass doors
into the wild ever-blue aura of Montana—
perma-perfumed with essential oils of
moss, glacier, pine, punched
with trout-scented beads of river.

I did not know
that I could live
to be seventy.
Each night was the only one—vast
black pulled at me.

Five decades later
I grasp the risk—
alone with the evening's cash
wilderness camping with Dog
navigating my little rusty car with bad tires
along mountains of empty highway.

Cornbread Magic

The best cornbread I ever ate was claimed by its maker messed up.
It was greasy and hard as peanut brittle.
See—it don't matter how it turns out.
It might be flat, fluffy, crumpled or solid as a hockey puck.
Filling up on cornbread is like going to church.

Can you scrounge up an old iron skillet?
Have you got some ancestors?
It helps to call on them. Let one sit on each shoulder.

You'll need some grease.
Bacon fat, lard, butter, or fancy oil.
An egg or two is nice if the hens are layin'.

Pour in some sweet, goat, canned, or buttermilk—
or water if you're plum broke that day—or
yogurt if you've come a long way.

There's white or yellow cornmeal—
probably other colors I don't know about
that self-rising Martha is good, too.

Bake it at 425 or near. Use a recipe or not. It's ok if people debate that.
Fry, pancake or fritter it. Just let it bake 'til it smells done.
Let the aroma holler your name!

Cornmeal is the root of your being and will work with you!

Eat it with beans, grill it for jelly.
Yes, you can stuff it in your glass of milk and eat it with a spoon.

Cut it in squares or triangles, or let a teenager go crazy cutting shapes
if they agree not to sculpt obscene body parts.

Just don't make it sweet.

Witness

Mom shoved cabbage
down the throat of a Mason jar
her forearm and fist a fit
she held its squeaky
mouth with a hooked thumb
slid the strap sharp
knife deep
jamming it up and down
chopping finer
cramming crunching—

move she scolded *in case the knife slips*

I nudged close again
knick and blood
jitters till at last she poured saltwater
set the jars in the water bath
jingled and clinking against each other

the 1950s gas stove
belted out a flame the
kitchen boiled—

she told the scalding oatmeal story
how it killed Dad's baby sister
a hog scraping where the
cauldron spilled on a boy—

she growled *move honey*

bedtime—worrisome pillow
pop-gun sounds
lids sealing sauerkraut.

Watermelon Salt

House is as hot as a cracker box
Mommy would say.

Near evening,
a watermelon rolled its meaty
seedy ready self to the mud pie kitchen
slashed open, sprinkled with salt.

Juice rivers through the day's play dirt
plunge off elbow waterfalls
heads crowned by slices
skin sticky, hair crusty
from watermelon salt.

Twilight cools to nightfall,
lightning bug catch 'em games—
mosquitos bite toes, thickened
gummy- bathed in watermelon salt.

Shivering itching scratching
blanket wrapping
Dad shows me how to find the Big Dipper.

Fearing Martians, girls become philosophers.
When will the moon end?
Is the world made of cheese?
You're going to marry Elvis?

Beyond our maple shelter
owls hoot premonitions.
Child life is sweet-salty.

Copperheads

Granny met us at the car
wearing her pinstripe
public nurse uniform
when we came to visit from Ohio.

She spat shrill warnings—

Now you watch out for them snakes!
Theys swarming under that tobaccy dryin in the barn!

Them cliffs are a nest of reptiles
just waiting for a briggity-britches!

The Little Sandy River Gorge offered
caves and belly-laying views over the rim.

I hear her screech as I climb the fence—

Your legs gonna swell black and need amputation!
I swear Cleo she's snuck off!

In the cow-pied briars,
Annie Oakley and me
silver gun, fringed holster,
stay alert for the secret
cucumber stink of copperheads.

Corn

Aunt Violet's truck
careened on a curve out of
Sandy Hook toward Isonville
and dumped her with a load
of coal into a ravine,
leaving her mind wrong.

She lived with her mommy after that,
in the house on stilts.

The two
vanilla-scented old ladies
matched like a sweater twin-set.
Us kids couldn't tell them apart
and called them both Granny.

They were tall and boney,
wore long dresses,
rolled their cornsilk hair
into tight muffin buns at the neck,
and smoked cob pipes.

They kept a free-range cow,
tossed dried corn to the chickens
that scratched under the house,
and lived like benign trolls
beside a crick.

The laying out of Granny Alice
was a featherbed
as warm as a kitten,
was a feast of puffy white cake
on a corn-flowered plate.

Mom, 1980

The funeral director said,
you will never forget her
in the coffin, so she should look pretty.

Good luck, I said. Not much to work with.
We three sisters explode, laughing crying.

He approves the mauve dress.
Pink reminds us of life—the wig
makes the package less shocking.

Someone made a joke about a bad hair day—
chokes sobs a snotty pile
seeping tissue wads.

We draw the line at the corpse wearing glasses,
but couldn't stop the hysterics.
He assured us it was normal.

We always worried about being normal.

Evening visitation, too many flowers
little bouquets made for the children.

I wedge a tight bud in her stiff fist.
The following day it is a fully blossomed rose.

Ironweed

> "Hear me out: that which you call death
> I remember."
>> Louise Glück, *The Wild Iris*

After greenhouse annuals have delighted
spring wishers in planned gardens
I'm late-blooming ironweed a
perennial untended challenged by
tidy lawns and weed killer.

Wild roots willed deep
nursed on a fence post
boned my legs, arms
bit through clay, ate rock

each of my years found sun—
and rebirthed purple on a tough stalk.

Marriage and a Frog

I rousted the fight breakfast
targeting your criminal machine whacking
    wildflower beheading
        critter habitat destruction.

But YOU
gassed up behemoth mower
    and whipped up a clipping
        twister as sharp as razors.

Come evening
I found Giant Bullfrog
    paralyzed on the battlefield
        dissected, still breathing

a wide flat sliver of gray meat
sliced precisely across his back,
    like a live victim study
        of muscles, tendons, nerve ganglia.

I grabbed a baseball bat,
demanded suffering's end.

You said you felt bad,
then beat Giant Bullfrog to death.

Laurel Gorge Cultural Center
Sandy Hook Kentucky

Red farm gate locked,
arms crossed against Covid-19—
my search for historical evidence denied.

Across the road, the Little Sandy River bumps
over falls and rocks, gurgling up creamed coffee.

I long for the time I could have sipped,
learned from aunts and grandmas
sharing troubles, laughing out fears.

My mom would twinkle at the changes—
medium-security prison
medical center
motel
McDonald's.

I am grateful for the things that didn't change—
green hills, dialect, family names.

I explain who I am—
Oh honey, that makes us cousins!

I smell bones in the ground.
The echo has gone quiet.

I need the way my being wrings
itself out and hangs the
nonsense on the clothesline for a good airing.

My kin nearby
knock around in their graves.

Thank You!

Dale Farmer and Sherrie Skipper, my Mystic Taters, my loving witnesses, without you, I'm just pecans.

To the poet Pauletta Hansel for helping me define the character of my topic and my voice as Appalachian. Through her groups and classes, I created the first early draft of this book.

Thanks to my sister Paula Roberts for not letting me get too big for my britches and my sister Tana Eiler for frequent fact-checks.

Thanks to my friend, the photographer Ron Stevens, for his generosity, and to Becki Ison for her project photos of Isonville.

The saying goes that *when the student is ready, the teacher will come;* that teacher would be Sherry Cook Stanforth, whose excitement gave me courage. Thanks for the excellent timing!

Thanks to my husband Roland Kalbli, for putting up with a lot.

Jackie Ison Kalbli's family migrated to Butler County, Ohio, from Elliott County, Kentucky, in 1950 during a period when jobs in construction, auto, and industry lured folks from Appalachia in the hope of better lives. As a child, she was an outsider, a hillbilly, a briar. She worked hard to erase evidence of that heritage, such as dialect, because it was identified with ignorance. Food customs were hidden. Visits to Kentucky were few. Now, as an elder, she celebrates and elevates all things coming out of the hills and hollers. A pilgrimage often takes her to Isonville or Sandyhook, where she looks for clues and relatives but mostly finds graves. She appreciates the inner Kentuckian that she is and grieves the loss of those connections. Jackie concluded a teaching career that spanned 38 years and is now retired but is still happiest at school.

She earned two Bachelor's Degrees at the University of Cincinnati, an M.Ed. at Miami University, and an MFA in Poetry at Ashland University in Ohio. She lives in Oxford, Ohio, with her husband. She grows weeds, tomatoes, peppers and plants trees. At age 73, *Ironweed* is her first chapbook.

www.ingramcontent.com/pod-product-compliance
Lightning Source LLC
Chambersburg PA
CBHW022106080426
42734CB00009B/1496